MIKE SMALLEY

7 LIES
CHRISTIANS
BELIEVE
ABOUT
THE LOST

7 LIES CHRISTIANS BELIEVE ABOUT THE LOST

Copyright © 2003 by Mike Smalley

ISBN: **0-9718254-2-4**

Cover Design: Joe Potter, Potter Design *www.joepotter.com*

DEDICATION

This book is dedicated to my maternal grandparents. They never wrote a book, so I read their lives. To myself and those who know them, they truly wrote a bestseller. No boy ever had better heroes. No man ever had greater friends.

TABLE OF CONTENTS

FOREWORD

No one likes to think that they are believing a lie. However, lies are often easier to believe than the truth. The sad fact is that we can even gravitate to a lie rather than embrace the truth.

Imagine if we proposed to gather tens of thousands of Christians together and have a time of worship. Nothing but God-glorifying worship...a multitude in one place to raise their hands and sing glorious praises to God. What an incredible blessing it would be.

How about we then (after the worship) go to the nearest gathering of sinners and share our faith with them? Not such a good feeling. In fact, such thoughts can even make palms sweat. Yet that's what we have been commissioned to do – to preach the Gospel to every creature despite our very real fears. As long as we listen to lies about our inadequacy, etc., rather than such truths as "I can do all things through Christ who strengthens me," we will never get this most necessary of jobs done.

The lie of inadequacy feathers the bed of complacency. Moses, Gideon, Jeremiah, Paul, etc., all felt inadequate for the task God had for them, but they conquered their fears through faith in His wonderful promises. We must do the same.

Mike Smalley can help you conquer your fears. Not only is he a personal friend, but I trust him as a man of God because I have seen that his mouth matches his pen. He walks as he talks. The principles of this book will greatly help you. Run with them while there is still time.

– *Ray Comfort, Evangelist*

PREFACE

Lies hurt people, lies hurt organizations, and lies hurt the church. Jesus said He was the way, the truth and the life and that Satan was the father of all lies.

It is obvious, even to the most casual observer, that the modern-day church has been deceived, and that she has grown cold in her efforts and zeal to reach the lost.

Bill Bright, founder of Campus Crusade for Christ, in his book, The Coming Revival, states from his research that only 2% of professing Christians share their faith regularly. The reasons for this are too numerous to mention here. One of those reasons is very clear - we have been lied to.

One of my callings as an evangelist is to "equip the saints for the work of the ministry." Jesus said the truth would set us free. I pray this book serves as a fresh call to arms to motivate you to make the "Great Commission" the "Great Completion" in our generation.

Satan knows the potential of an on-fire believer. He knows that if he convinces us of these lies, a generation will not hear the Gospel. I am determined that will not happen in my generation. If we expose those lies, that can't happen. He knows your potential!

CHAPTER ONE

Lie#1:

"Their eternal destination is already decided."

I was standing in my home in the mid 1990s with a Christian neighbor. Our wives were enjoying a time of fellowship, while Eric and I discussed the things of God. The conversation quickly turned to evangelism, and Eric shared with me about a church with an outrageous teaching. This congregation had embraced a belief of radical predestination.

For centuries, certain men have taught a radical predestination, meaning that God, in eternity's past, has decided who will go to Heaven and who will go to Hell. They actually *refuse* to share Christ with anyone, believing it is a complete waste of their time.

This is a totally absurd teaching. It robs one of a reward for being obedient, and it takes away the ability for God to punish. If disobedience were preprogrammed by God, then how could God hold the person accountable for being disobedient? God had programmed him to be disobedient.

If I have been predestined to be a follower of Jesus and to

11

obey the commands of the Lord, how can God reward me for the obedience He caused in the first place?

If I can't help but turn my back on God, there is no justification for sending me to Hell. If I can't help but be a Christian, there would be no reward in Heaven. So we end up with a belief that our choices simply don't matter.

Philosophies like this have dealt repeated blows to the advancement of the Gospel. If the eternity of everyone is already decided, then every pastor, missionary, and others in the ministry are fools. Why preach the Gospel? How absurd it would be for a person to leave their home, their family, and their occupation and preach the Gospel to people when it ultimately doesn't matter!

If God has predetermined where people will go after they die and they have no choice in the matter, then numerous scriptures in the Old and New Testaments become obsolete.

While I was attending a prayer meeting with the late Leonard Ravenhill, he reminded us, "The Bible is either absolute or it's all obsolete." In other words, it either is a divine book without errors, or it is not.

Consider the following:

"I call heaven and earth to record this day against you, that I have set before you life and death, blessing and cursing: therefore **choose** *life, that both thou and thy seed may live."* (Deuteronomy 30:19, emphasis mine)

"And if it seem evil unto you to serve the Lord, **choose** *you this day whom ye will serve; whether the gods which your fathers served that were on the other side of the flood, or the gods of the Amorites, in whose land ye dwell: but as for me and my house, we will serve the Lord."* (Joshua 24: 15, emphasis mine)

"...the soul that sinneth, it shall die." (Ezekiel 18:4b)

"For the wages of sin is death; but the gift of God is eternal life through Jesus Christ our Lord." (Romans 6:23)

The Bible, from beginning to end, indicates that man has been given a choice. Different terms expressing the right to choose are used over 4,000 times in scripture.

From the very beginning in the Garden of Eden, God gave instructions to Adam and Eve about the tree, and then let the choice of their obedience be up to them.

In the last chapter of the Bible, Jesus says in Revelation 22:17b *"...whosoever will, let him take the water of life freely."*

It doesn't say "whoever is predestined..." **It clearly indicates a choice.**

Consider Lot's Wife

No two cities are more famous in ancient history than Sodom and Gomorrah. Sodom and Gomorrah were thriving cities that God destroyed because of their great wickedness. The destruction of Sodom is detailed in Genesis 19 where we are told that two angels sent by God came to visit Lot.

Genesis records that Lot took the angels home with him. In the evening the men of the city, both young and old, surrounded the house and demanded that the angels be brought out in order to have sexual relations with them. The end result of this is that the entire crowd was struck with blindness

Following this act of judgment, the angels said to Lot in verse 12: *"Have you anyone else here? Son-in-law, your sons, your daughters, and whomever you have in the city – take them out of this place! For we will destroy this place, because the outcry against them has grown great before the face of the Lord, and the Lord has sent us to destroy it"* (NKJV).

In verses 15 and 16, once again the angels say to Lot, *"Arise, take your wife and your two daughters who are here, lest you be consumed in the punishment of the city. And while he lingered, the men took hold of his hand, his wife's hand, and the hands of his two daughters, the Lord being* **merciful** *to him and brought him and set him outside the city. So it came to pass when they had brought them outside, that he said, 'Escape for your life! Do not look behind you nor stay anywhere in the plain. Escape to the mountains, lest you be destroyed'"* (NKJV).

What mercy the Lord showed Lot and his family! He forewarned Lot and his family of his intention to destroy the city, even sending two angels to personally communicate the warning. They even physically led them out of the city by hand! Clearly, the Bible shows us that Lot had a choice whether to obey the word of the Lord through His messengers. Verse 26 tells us, *"But his wife looked back behind him, and she became a pillar of salt"* (NKJV).

Obviously, Lot's wife made a choice to look back on that which God was bringing her out of. Lot's wife is a picture and a testimony to the generations that have followed since, that God has sent by His mercy, messengers to lead us by the *hand* out of sin and death.

Notice that the Bible does not say that they led them by their neck, but by their *hand*. They had their own free will, but Lot's wife turned and looked back. So it is with us - we have a choice.

Korah's Rebellion

In Numbers 16, we are given the story of Korah's rebellion against Moses and his brother Aaron on their way to the Promised Land. Korah was unhappy with Moses' leadership and had recruited 250 leaders among the people to confront Moses. God's anger was consumed against Korah and the men who had joined with him in rebellion against Moses, the man of God.

Under the leadership of the Holy Spirit, Moses spoke to the congregation in Numbers 16:26 and said, *"Depart now from the tents of these wicked men! Touch nothing of theirs, lest you be consumed in all their sins"* (NKJV).

Their response is recorded in verse 27, *"So they got away from around the tents of Korah, Dathan, and Abiram..."* (NKJV).

God clearly gave these men a choice, "You can die with these rebellious men or you can choose to live." And wisely, they chose to separate themselves. It was a very good thing that they did, for the Bible tells us in verse 32 that *"the earth opened its mouth and swallowed them up..."* (NKJV).

Predestination vs. Foreknowledge

Many people confuse these two terms. Predestination involves God making a choice for certain individuals. While there are instances of predestination in the scripture, they do not deal with the souls of individuals.

Israel was predestined by God to be His chosen people. Jerusalem was predestined by God to be the place where Jesus died. When the Bible speaks of predestination, it speaks about issues of place and timing - not individuals' souls.

God, in His foreknowledge (His ability to know the future), knows who will make a decision to accept Him or reject Him, but He has never made that choice for an individual.

This makes the preaching of the Gospel even more urgent as the Bible says in Romans 10:14,15a, *"How then shall they call on him in who they have not believed? and how shall they believe in him of whom they have not heard? and how shall they hear without a preacher? and how shall they preach, except they be sent?"*

Recognizing the lie of eternal predestination, let us sharpen the sword of urgency to cut through our comfort zone and do all we can to reach the lost with the Gospel. If you really believe that Jesus Christ could come back to the earth at any moment, then you have to believe that we have *minutes* to reach *billions*.

Every individual deserves the right to accept or reject the Gospel on the basis of reality.

Consider the Disciples

Jesus' twelve disciples didn't seem to believe in predestination, considering the fact that eleven of the twelve of them were killed for preaching the Gospel. Many of them died on foreign soil.

Paul took three missionary journeys around the then-known world for the simple purpose of proclaiming the Gospel. Men who literally walked with Jesus would have been outright fools to have paid such a high price if they had known their efforts were in vain anyway.

Many Christians have been led to believe that the choices of other people in regards to the Gospel is none of their business. This is completely unscriptural, and a practice that Jesus did not model.

The Bible says in Matthew 4:23, *"And Jesus went about **all** Galilee, **teaching… and preaching** the gospel of the kingdom, and healing all manner of sickness and all manner of disease among the people"* (emphasis mine).

Jesus' disciples learned this principle from Him and modeled their lives likewise. *"Therefore they that were scattered abroad **went everywhere** preaching the word."* (Acts 8:4, emphasis mine)

Paul never considered the idolaters' religion in Athens to be "none of his business." He proclaimed loudly in the public streets, *"Ye men of Athens, I perceive that in all things ye are too superstitious. For as I passed by, and beheld your devotions, I found an altar with this* inscription, *TO THE UNKNOWN GOD. Whom therefore ye ignorantly worship, him declare I unto you"* (Acts 17:22-23).

Paul declared again in 2 Corinthians 5:11 *"Knowing therefore the terror of the Lord, we persuade men."*

The verse does not say, "Recognizing the right to people's privacy, we keep our mouths shut and simply live the Gospel."

In the American justice system, it is a crime to observe a tragedy and fail to render aid. If you see your neighbor's house on fire, you don't say, "It's none of my business to go over and wake him up."

If you see a young man drowning, you don't say "I really shouldn't get into other people's business."

Jesus made it our business when He said, "If you love me keep my commandments." And He then commanded us, *"Go ye into* **ALL** *the world, and preach the gospel to* **every creature.** *He that* **believeth** *and is baptized shall be saved; but he that* **believeth not** *shall be damned"* (Mark 16:15-16 , emphasis mine).

The fact is, Jesus commanded us to go into all the world and preach the Gospel because mankind's eternal destination *has not* been decided. People who have no desire to see the lost saved are, in the words of the late Charles Spurgeon, "not saved themselves."

If you believe the Bible is true about choice, than you understand that lost mankind is headed for eternity in hell. Unless believers step out of their comfort zones and share the Gospel with the sinners within their circle of opportunity.

CHAPTER TWO

Lie#2:

"Jesus gave grace to everyone."

I consider the greatest lie Satan has sold the church to be the lie that Jesus gave grace to everyone.

Both now and when Jesus was physically on the earth, grace is and was available to everyone. However, Jesus did not then, nor does He today, give grace to everyone.

The Bible clearly teaches us that Biblical evangelism is law to the proud and *grace to the humble.*

Consider the following:

"The law of the Lord is perfect, converting the soul..." (Psalm 19:7).

The Bible clearly states that the law of the Lord is perfect for converting the soul. Now we know that repentance through faith in the cross of Christ is the only means available for a man to be saved, so what exactly does this verse mean?

What is the Law?

The word *law* brings a puzzled reaction to most Christians. We know that the Old Testament law, i.e., sacrifices, ceremonies etc., found their fulfillment in the death, burial, and resurrection of Jesus, and do not apply to those living after the resurrection of Christ.

However, Jesus said in Matthew 5:17 that He did not come to destroy the law, but to fulfill it. So clearly the moral aspects of God's law have not changed.

The backbone of God's law is the Ten Commandments. As a matter of fact, Jesus Himself, during the sermon on the mount, quotes nine of the ten commandments.

Paul understood the vital importance of using the law of God.

Consider the following:

"Now we know that whatever the law says, it says to those who are under the law, **that every mouth may be stopped,** *and all* **the world may become guilty before God"** (Romans 3:19 NKJV).

"What shall we say then? Is the law sin? God forbid. Nay, I had not known sin, but by the law: for I had not known lust, except the law had said, 'thou shalt not covet" (Romans 7:7).

"Wherefore the law was our schoolmaster to bring us unto Christ, that we might be justified by faith" (Galatians 3:24).

Notice what the Holy Spirit said through Paul in Romans 3:19. The law of the Lord has a two-fold function: (1) to shut every mouth and (2) to show the world that they are guilty before God.

Considering Jesus' Example

LAW TO THE PROUD

In Luke 10:25, the Bible says, *"...a certain lawyer stood up, and tempted him, sayin, Master, what shall I do to inherit eternal life?"* Notice Jesus' response in the next verse (26) He said to him, *"What is written in the law? how readest thou?"*

Knowing the man was tempting Him and that he was asking with a proud heart, Jesus did not give the man grace. He gave the man law. Verse 27 records the man's answer to Jesus' question. Jesus acknowledged that the man had answered rightly. In verse 29, the scripture says *"But he, willing to justify himself, said unto Jesus, And who is my neighbour?"* If you are standing in the presence of the Son of God who has come to die on the cross for your sins, is it pride or humility to justify yourself in His sight? It is obviously pride!

I am not saying that Jesus did not radically love this man. For clearly, He loved him so much that He had come to die for him. Jesus loved him with the law, because the law is our *schoolmaster* that brings us to Christ.

This teacher was an expert in God's law and his knowledge of that left him empty and brought him to the Savior. But he had not come humbly; he had come proudly. He had not allowed the law to work its proper purpose in his heart to bring humility and a sense of his own wickedness and sinfulness.

Instead, he came to Jesus with the same opinion that many do today - that there are plenty of people worse than they are, and that their knowledge of Bible truths means they *have* the truth of the Bible.

Friends, there are millions today who think church is about going to a building each week and hearing a sermon about God. The truth is that we come to church to meet the God the sermon is all about.

Many people (even Satan) know *the Word of God*, but they do not know *the God of the Word*.

Following the proud man's response, Jesus then proceeded to

tell the man the parable of the Good Samaritan in order to expose that he did not love his neighbor as himself.

Because he did not love his neighbor as himself, he was a violator of the second commandment. He also could not keep the first which was to love God above all else. This man loved himself first, and hated Samaritans. How can a man say he loves God with all he has if he does not love his neighbor?

"If a man say, I love God, and hateth his brother, he is a liar: for he that loveth not his brother whom he hath seen, how can he love God whom he hath not seen?" (1 John 4:20)

Jesus did not give this man grace because he was not humble. By giving him the law of God, Jesus was placing him in the path of having his "mouth shut" and proving that he was "guilty before God." It was the man's choice to walk away without repentance. Jesus loved him with the truth.

The Rich Young Ruler

Another example of "law to the proud" is in Luke 18:18-21. *"A certain ruler asked him, saying, Good Master, what shall I do to inherit eternal life?" And Jesus said unto him, Why callest thou me good? None is good except one, that is God. Thou knowest the commandments, Do not commit adultery, Do not kill, Do not steal, Do not bear false witness."* And the ruler said, *"I have kept all of these since my youth."*

Notice again, Jesus uses law toward a proud young man. Is it pride or humility to tell Jesus you have never sinned? Is it pride or humility to hear Him recite the commandments and still tell Him you have never broken them, and that from childhood on, you were essentially as good as Jesus Himself? Again, we see a prevailing pattern. The young man was convinced of his own goodness, and that there were plenty of people worse than himself!

Jesus gave the man law to cultivate the same fruit in him that we discussed earlier with the man in Luke 10. Jesus always gave law to the proud. However, He gave grace to those who were humble. This principle is reaffirmed in James 4:6 *"...God resiseth the proud, but giveth grace unto the humble."*

If we are to follow in the footsteps of Jesus as true and faithful witnesses, we must follow His example.

GRACE TO THE HUMBLE
Nicodemus

In John 3, we have the story of Nicodemus, a Pharisee. He was a teacher of the law of God and had studied it diligently for years. Nicodemus came to Jesus with a humble heart. How do we know? Listen to his words.

"Rabbi, we know that thou art a teacher come from God: for no man can do these miracles that thou doest, except God be with him" (John 3:2).

Nicodemus sought after Jesus for a private interview. He did not ask any questions upon his initial approach, but merely came and blurted out his acknowledgment that Jesus truly was sent from the Father. Jesus did not need to give the law to him. Nicodemus was already humble.

Jesus responded to Nicodemus in verse 3, *"...unless one is born again, he cannot see the kingdom of God"* (KNJV). In other words, Nicodemus was close, but not quite there. So Jesus gave him a message of grace, of how to make right what was wrong in his life.

The Adulterous Woman

When Jesus encountered the woman caught in the act of adultery, she bowed humbly before His presence. She never asked why they did not attempt to stone the man with whom who she had committed adultery. She never accused those in the crowd of being hypocrites, nor did she try to accuse others whom she knew had committed similar crimes.

The woman merely stood, guilty in the eyes of man and guilty by the law of God. Humbly, she knew the punishment for such a crime was death and that by the law she was guilty and deserved it. Thus, in her humility, she offered no objections to the punishment being carried out.

Imagine this woman's glorious surprise when Jesus came forward and did not give her law, but grace. He asked, *"Woman, where are your accusers...neither do I condemn thee. Go and sin no more."* Jesus didn't give her law. He gave her grace because she was humble.

Woman at the Well

In John 4, Jesus begins a conversation with a woman at a well. He quickly exposes that He is aware she is living in open adultery. In humility, she confesses that His comments are accurate and quickly runs to bring the men of her city to the well and to the feet of Jesus. Many were soundly saved on that day because of her humility.

Satan knows that the only key the Holy Spirit has given to prepare the heart for grace is God's law. It is what the Holy Spirit uses to "shut every mouth" and show their "guilt before God." Only guilty people plead for mercy.

Charles Spurgeon said, "Men will never accept grace until they tremble before a just and Holy law."

Martin Luther, in his commentary on Galatians, recognized that one of Satan's greatest lies was that the law of God was not necessary when sharing the Gospel.

JESUS GAVE GRACE TO EVERYONE

"Satan, the god of all dissention, stirreth up daily, new sects, and last of all, which of all other I should never have foreseen or once suspected, he has raised up a sect such as teach...that men should not be terrified by the law, but gently exhorted by the preaching of the grace of Christ."

Luther, the great reformer and leader of the Reformation, understood the necessity of God's law to prepare the listener for the Gospel message. And he instructed that to depart from that teaching was to have followed the lie and doctrine of Satan himself.

When we give grace to a proud sinner, it serves only to further harden him to the Gospel. When a sinner is not convinced of his need of God's forgiveness, it will be offensive to him to imply that he needs God's forgiveness. Like the men in the Bible, he, too, believes that there are plenty of people worse than he is. God's Word proves differently. Jesus said there was no one good but God, and He then used the commandments to illustrate His point.

Consider the Quotes of Other Great Men from History

"**Before** I can preach love, mercy and grace, I must preach sin, law, and judgment."

– *John Wesley*

"Lower the law and you dim the light by which man perceives his guilt. This is a very serious loss to the sinner than a gain, for it lessens the likelihood of his conviction and conversion. I say that you have **deprived** the Gospel of its ablest auxiliary (its most powerful weapon).

"When you have set aside the law, you have taken away from it the schoolmaster that is to bring men to Christ. **I do not believe** that any man can preach the Gospel who does not preach the law."

– Charles Spurgeon

Satan trembles at the thought of a Christian church or nation that understands law to the proud and grace to the humble. By returning to the Biblical pattern of evangelism set forth by Jesus, we will accelerate the harvest of the 21st century!

CHAPTER THREE

Lie#3:

"Nobody would believe me."

Every honest Christian has wrestled with this issue at one time or another. Jeremiah was told not to be afraid of people's faces. He was obviously struggling with the fear of man, and perhaps his own believability.

Numerous people in the Bible resisted the call to deliver God's message for their day. For example:

Moses

When Moses was visited by God at the burning bush in Exodus 3, he asked God numerous questions. Perhaps you can identify with the questions Moses asked.

"And Moses said unto God, Who am I, that I should go unto Pharaoh, and that I should bring forth the children of Israel out of Egypt?" (Exodus 3:11)

"...What shall I say unto them?" (Exodus 3:13b)

"And Moses answered and said, But, behold, they will not believe me..." (Exodus 4:1)

"And Moses said unto the Lord, O my Lord, I am not eloquent...but I am slow of speech and of a slow tongue." (Exodus 4:10)

What was the bottom line response of God to Moses' questions? The same response He gives to us today when we ask the same questions Moses asked. *"Now therefore go, and I will be with thy mouth and teach thee what thou shalt say."* (Exodus 4:12)

Gideon

Gideon was a young man at a critical time in Israel's history. When the Lord spoke to Gideon and told him he would be used to save Israel from the hand of his enemies, his response was *"...Oh my Lord, wherewith shall I save Israel? behold, my family is poor in Manasseh, and I am the least in my father's house"* (Judges 6:15).

Titus

Titus was a spiritual son of the Apostle Paul. They had labored together on numerous occasions and at some point in their ministry, Paul left Titus on the Island of Crete. Overwhelmed by the task of establishing the Gospel on the island, Titus had written to Paul asking him why he had left him there on that island. I believe Titus was a confident young man when he was with Paul, but now faced with ministry on his own, Satan began to shoot darts of doubt and discouragement into his mind.

Why am I here?

What good can I do?

I am only a young man. Who will believe me?

Paul responds to Titus' questions in Titus 1:5, *"For this reason I left you in Crete, that you should set in order the things that are lacking, and appoint elders in every city..."* (NKJV).

Think about what Paul was saying in this passage. Not only was Titus going to preach the Gospel, but his preaching was going to produce converts. Those converts were going to produce churches. Those churches would need elders to oversee them.

At the time of Paul's writing to Titus, none of the above was in place. Paul had confidence in Titus. People would believe his preaching and the results would last for eternity.

Clearly, Satan gains a great foothold in our lives when he can convince us to keep silent the message God has given us for our family, friends and the lost to whom God sends us.

Satan doesn't want you to realize that you really are believable! He doesn't want you to understand and walk in the reality that the Word of God in your mouth is life. He doesn't want you to grasp the truth that the Word of the Lord in you is not going to return void and that "the same spirit that raised Christ from the dead dwells in you." He doesn't want you to get hold of the fact that "the power of life and death is in the power of your tongue" and when you speak life, it changes things. He doesn't want people to know that you can lay hands on the sick and they will recover.

Consider what Jesus says about His Church

He will never leave you.

"Lo, I am with you always." (Matt. 28:20)

You will be given the right words to speak.

"But when they deliver you up, take no thought how or what ye shall

speak: for it shall be given you in that same hour what ye shall speak. For it is not ye that speak, but the Spirit of your Father which speaketh in you" (Matthew 10:19-20).

The Word does not return void.

"So shall my word be that goeth forth out of my mouth: it shall not return unto me void, but it shall accomplish that which I please, and it shall prosper in the thing whereto I sent it" (Isaiah 55:11).

Jesus told His disciples, "Follow Me and I will make you fishers of men." This was the first call in scripture to the disciples to come and follow the Lord, obviously with the goal of spreading the good news around the world. The application is very clear. Jesus asks us to come and follow Him, and He will teach us to be fishers of men. So our responsibility is to respond to the call to follow and His responsibility is to make us into fishers of men.

Rise to the occasion! There are people who won't step out of darkness until you show up. Satan knows this. He fights it. He organizes and strategizes events and thoughts that will keep you in fear, but greater is He that is in you than he that is in the world. Jesus sent us into the world *knowing* people *would* believe us. Romans 1: 16 says, *"For I am not ashamed of the gospel of Jesus Christ: for it is the* **power of God** *unto salvation to everyone that* **believeth"** (emphasis mine).

The Gospel itself is the power of God. It does not *contain* the power of God. It *is* the power of God. The Gospel being presented is God's power in action!

30

7 reasons Satan wants you to believe the lie, "No one will believe your message."

1. **It destroys your motivation.** When your motivation is destroyed, you never get out of the boat to walk on the water.

2. **It puts seeds of doubt in your heart which can spread to every other area of your faith.** Doubt is extremely contagious

3. **It creates the belief that you have no purpose in your life.**

4. **It will produce frustration.** The enemy knows if you don't live in the calling that God has placed on your life, you cannot experience the peace and joy that come from sharing the Great Commission with those around you.

5. **Satan knows that if he can silence your witness, he has silenced the witness of those you would have led to Christ.** Satan knows very well that the Gospel is spread through multiplication! He sees far more into the future than the average Christian.

6. **If you are convinced that no one will believe you, the load of the Great Commission will then fall to even fewer workers, resulting in fewer conversions to Christ.**

7. **It guarantees that no one will look to you as a mentor and duplicate your soul winning efforts.**

You have incredible potential in the hands of an awesome God. From the moment of your birth, God was planning and desiring to take your talents and your giftings and use them for His glory if you would only let Him.

I believe with all of my heart that every Christian has talents and gifts that others would pay money to obtain. Stewardship for the Christian is not only a financial issue, but it covers every area of our lives. We are stewards of the talents, giftings, and uniqueness of our personalities. Use them for His glory.

Never underestimate your influence on the life of another. Hundreds, even thousands, are influenced directly or indirectly by the words you speak each day.

Remember, only one man invented electricity, only one man developed the smallpox vaccine, and only one man led the German army to annihilate eight million innocent people. Never underestimate the power of *one*. You are that one in the hands of a mighty God. You are believable! The Gospel is the power of God through you. Allow Him to use you today as an "arrow of His love."

CHAPTER FOUR

Lie#4:

"The key to reaching people is simply living the Gosepl in front of them."

Many people believe a godly lifestyle is enough to reach people for Christ. While Jesus did say that people would know we belonged to Him by our love for one another, the verse does not say that by this, all men shall become convicted of their sins. The verse does not say that by this, all men shall ask for a savior. It simply says that men will know that *you* are a Christian.

Many people believed Jesus was the Son of God. Thousands saw Him perform many miracles and live a perfect life. **For 33 years, people had total perfection in their midst, but it did not result in masses of conversions.** In fact, the majority called for His death. If Jesus' perfect life did not result in overwhelming salvations, why would we who are very imperfect believe that our *imperfect* lives will have better results?

A very popular saying from years ago is, "Preach the Gospel and, whenever possible, use words." These kinds of expressions sound safe, but in reality they are not completely scriptural. While it is true that many people say one thing and do another, Jesus assumed that if we loved Him, we would keep His commandments, and He clearly commanded each person who follows Him to open his mouth and speak!

"Go ye into all the world, and preach the gospel..." (Mark 16:15).

The Bible says in Romans that the Gospel is the power of God unto salvation to everyone who believes.

One of the reasons that many believers are frustrated and even discouraged from sharing their faith in Christ is that they have not used the Biblical methods to do so. This has led to frustration and stagnation in the area of personal evangelism.

Understanding the Gospel

The Bible says only *the Gospel* is the power of God unto salvation.

Many sincere Christians think sharing the Gospel means giving your testimony or telling stories from the Bible.

IT IS NOT!!

These are all necessary parts of the *Christian message*, but they are not "the Gospel."

The word *Gospel* simply means "good news," but in order for "good news" to be good, it must be an improvement on the news we have previously received.

For example, if someone were to enthusiastically say to you, "The oxygen in the air is safe to breathe," that would not be good news, but simply common information. However, if thirty days prior to that conversation, chemical warfare had broken out and the air was hazardous to inhale, the above announcement from a newscaster or radio official would be good news because it is an *improvement* on previously given bad news.

The reason the Gospel is not good news to most sinners is that we have not been faithful to deliver the bad news first.

Paul outlined what sharing the Gospel should include in 1 Corinthians 15:1,3-6a: *"Moreover, brethren, I declare unto you the* **gospel** *which I preached unto you, which also ye have received, and wherein ye stand; For I delivered unto you first of all that which I also received, how that Christ died for our sins according to the scriptures; And that he was buried, and that he rose again the third day according to the scriptures: And that he was seen of Cephas, then of the twelve: After that he was seen of above five hundred brethren..."*

Notice the God-given pattern here. In order for a message to qualify as the Gospel, it must include the following elements:

1. Christ died.

The Gospel is not simply the "good news." It is the "good news" of Jesus Christ. It must be declared that Jesus Christ is the Son of God and that He died on the cross.

2. The message of personal sin.

The scripture says Jesus died for *our* sins. This must be made personal to every sinner. *He* has sinned. *He* has violated the commandments of God. *He* is imperfect and must be judged.

3. Jesus rose from the dead.

The story of Jesus' death, burial, and resurrection must be included if our message is to qualify as the Gospel. The fact that God raised Jesus from the dead documents that He was exactly who He claimed to be - the only begotten Son of God.

The Holy Spirit has promised that His power will rest when we share the Gospel. If our message does not include a message of sin, righteousness and judgment to come, there will be no conviction of the Holy Spirit. His power will be absent and we will not see lives changed. (John 16:7-11)

Yes, the Holy Spirit helps us to live the Gospel before a lost world. However, His promise to manifest His power only comes when we live a holy life and declare His holy message.

CHAPTER FIVE

Lie#5:

"People have heard the Gospel before and realize they are lost."

One of Satan's greatest achievements is deception.

Satan works hard at ensuring that people believe a lie. This does not have to be a preached doctrine or a proclaimed practice, but merely an "under the surface" belief - *a false assumption, or subtle lie*.

With the vast media and print outlets in western nations, it is tempting to believe that most people fully understand the Gospel, eternity, sin, and the wrath of God. Nothing could be further from the truth.

The Bible says in Hosea that God's people are *destroyed from lack of knowledge*. How much more are those who live in darkness!

Jesus said in John 3 that unless a man is born again, He cannot see kingdom of God.

The Great Commission is to go into all the world and declare the Gospel. Sinners do have a choice to accept or reject the Gospel. It is also true that once "all sinners" have been given a presentation of the Gospel by a Christian; the Great Commission has been completed. We are far from seeing that goal take place.

I remember speaking to a young man and asking him if he had heard of the Ten Commandments. Without being funny or trying to be smart, he simply said "No."

I can take you to the inner cities of America and introduce you to hundreds of children who have never heard a Bible story of Noah and the ark, Daniel and the lion's den, or baby Moses.

Once when I was a student, waiting for further instructions from a professor, I wrote the words to John 3:16 on a piece of paper. While others were finishing their exams, our professor was walking the aisles of the class. He looked down over my shoulder, saw the scripture written out, read it quietly and looked at me with the most bewildered expression and asked, "Is that true?" This was a man who was raised twenty miles outside of Dallas, Texas, who was in his forties and had never heard the message of John 3:16.

Years ago I was seated on an airplane next to a man in his thirties who had just moved from New York City to Dallas. The young man had grown up regularly attending a Catholic church, and had attended a private Catholic school from kindergarten through gaining his Bachelor's degree. His uncle was a high-ranking bishop in the New York Diocese.

Later in the conversation, this young man began to make fun of born-again Christians. (He did not yet know that I was a Christian or an evangelist!) To further stimulate the conversation, I inquisitively asked the young man "What is a born-again Christian?"

He replied, "Someone who has 'supposedly' had some kind of a super-spiritual experience with God." He said this smirking and laughing, obviously doubting the creditability of that of which he spoke.

I then asked the young man, "Have you ever heard the words

of Jesus in St. John 3:3? *"Except a man be born again, he cannot see the kingdom of God."* I will never forget the young man's reply.

After sixteen years of religious school, mass every week, and an uncle who was in the ministry, his reply was a simple, "No."

Think for a moment of your circle of influence – your co-workers, your neighbors, or even relatives, and current or former classmates. Can we safely assume that all of these people have received a proper presentation of the Gospel – that **ALL OF THEM** have been given an explanation of what sin is, and that it is not a disease that we catch, but a crime we commit?

Have they been warned that it is appointed unto man once to die and then the judgment?

Have they been told that Jesus said in Matthew 12 that we would give an account on the day of judgment of *every idle word* that we have spoken?

Has every sinner been warned? Has he been told that the book of Revelation declares that anyone whose name is not found recorded in the book of life will be cast into the Lake of Fire?

Has he been told that there is a way out and that Jesus is the way, the truth, and the life and that no man can come to the Father except through Him, and there has been no other name given under Heaven whereby men can be saved? Is it safe to assume that everyone in your circle is aware of these things? I think not.

One of Satan's greatest weapons is ignorance.

Remember the Bible teaches that natural man cannot receive the things of God. If the blind follow the blind, they will both fall into the ditch. In speaking of dating and marriage, Paul asked the question, "Can light have fellowship with darkness?" Here again is the irony – blindness, darkness, in other words, ignorance. "Blind" people do not have an understanding of the Gospel. The devil loves to keep them in ignorance. Unless a Christian, armed with the

Holy Spirit, brings light into that dark situation, that person has no chance of repenting and being saved.

Need further proof that all have not heard?

- Dr. David Barett reports in a recent "International Bulletin of Missionary Research" that the percentage of Christians in the world has remained substantially unchanged at 33%.

- He also states that some 4,000 people groups have no viable Christian witnesses.

- In 2001, 13.2 million people died without ever hearing the name of Jesus or the good news of Christ.

I recently returned from doing street evangelism with a Masters Commission team at the University of Texas in Austin, which is the largest university in America, boasting some 55,000 students.

After spending a day on the streets interviewing people about their beliefs, I was reminded once again, as I have been numerous times before, that *sinners don't see themselves as God sees them.*

Ruth Paxton, in her book, *Life on the Highest Plane*, reminds us of what the scripture says about the sinner. **Following is what the Bible says the attitude of the unsaved man is to God:**

- Galatians 4:8 – He does not know God.
- Romans 2:21 – He has no gratitude to God.
- Romans 3:11 – He has no desire for God.
- 1 John 4:10 – He has no love for God.
- John 3:18 – He has no faith in God.
- Romans 3:18 – He has no fear of God.

- Romans 1:21,25 – He does not worship God.
- 2 Timothy 3:8 – He resists the truth.
- 1 Corinthians 2:14 – He receives not the things of God.
- 2 Thessalonians 2:12 – He rejects God's truth.
- 2 Thessalonians 1:8 – He disobeys God's Gospel.
- Romans 5:10 – He is an enemy of God.

Let's look at the relationship of the unsaved man to God.

- Ephesians 2:17 – He is far from God.
- Romans 3:19 – He is guilty before God.
- John 3:18 – He is condemned by God.
- John 3:36 – He is under God's wrath.
- Ephesians 4:18 – He is alienated from the life of God.
- Ephesians 2:12 – He is without God in this life.
- 2 Thessalonians 1:9 – He is without God in the future.

I don't think an honest review of the above scriptures would cause anyone to disagree. The fact is, sinners don't see themselves as God sees them. They view themselves as *society* sees them. The average sinner believes there are plenty of people worse than he is. The average sinner believes that he is a good person.

Recently I asked a woman if she had ever told a lie. She said she had. She then admitted that made her a liar. She also admitted that she was a thief and that she has immoral thoughts. I then asked her if she still considered herself to be a good person. She broke into a large smile and honestly said to me, "Of course I am."

The Bible says in Proverbs 20:6 *"Most men will proclaim every one his own goodness..."* Yet from God's point of view there is none righteous, no not one. Isaiah says all of our righteous is like "filthy rags." Jesus said in Luke 18:19, *"there is none good but God."*

Let's try an experiment. Think for a moment of your closest unsaved friend or family member. Put that person in your mind. Picture their face; imagine the sound of their voice. Got it? Now, ask yourself the following question. Has God been angry with that person *every day* of their life? Not just some days, not just certain days - every day.

What's the answer?

Psalm 7:11, *"God judgeth the righteous, and God is angry with the* wicked **every day."**

That is a radically different view of God than most people know or think!

The God of this world is a God of love, but what does He love besides sinners? He loves grace. He loves mercy. He loves righteousness. He loves holiness. He loves justice and His law.

The fact is that you can be in love with someone and be angry with them at the same time. We don't have to look past our households to believe and understand that. God is no different in that regard. He has an indescribable love of humanity and yet the Bible declares that He is angry with the wicked every day.

I believe that if I asked the above true/false question to the average Christian in America, most Christians would say that God had not been angry with their unsaved friends every day - just some days.

I remember the story of the old Puritan preacher who was challenged by a street heckler. "Preacher" he said, "is it a sin for me to drink a beer?"

The wise preacher responded, "Sir, for you it is a sin to drink a glass of milk."

The man roared. The crowd laughed. "Why sir what kind of a narrow-minded religion do you follow that even milk is a sin?"

He replied, "Sir, you misunderstand me. I'm not saying it is a sin to drink a glass of milk, but I am saying that for you – you are a sinner, *you are sin*, your entire spirit is corrupted with it, your deeds are as filthy rags – and as long as you are a sinner, everything you do continues to hold you prisoner in a state of sin. When God sees you, He sees sin. When God sees you, He sees a sinner. No matter what you drink, your state before God does not change. You are a lost man on the brink of eternal damnation."

What a powerful illustration. May God once again, by His Holy Spirit, awaken the church to reply to the unsaved and use our hands, feet, and voices to declare these truths to sinners.

For how will men ask for grace unless they see that they are in danger? Only a drowning man reaches for a life jacket.

Biblical Examples

- In the story of Lazarus and the rich man, the rich man was lost while he lived, but he didn't know it. He went to Hell a surprised and dumbfounded man.

- In Luke 12, Jesus tells the story of a man consumed by greed who boasted of his accomplishments. But God said to him, *"This night thy soul shall be required of thee."* Obviously the implication of this is that he did not know his judgment was at hand. He died in ignorance.

Not one scripture in the Bible implies or indicates that sinners, left to themselves, understand their state before God. Paul said in Romans 7:7, *"I would not have known what sin was except through the law"* (NIV). In other words, he was ignorant and blinded until the glorious light of the Gospel shone on his conscience.

People confuse "believing in God" with "being right with God."

They confuse believing in the moral attributes and teachings of the Bible as being right with the God of the Bible.

They think going to a building once a week to hear a sermon about God makes them favored in His sight. They don't understand that the real goal is to meet and walk with the God the sermon is all about.

They confuse knowing the Word of God with knowing the God of the Word.

They live in great ignorance, believing that there are plenty of people worse than they are, and that God will forgive all their sins on Judgment Day. God will not forgive any sins *on* Judgment Day. He only forgives *before* Judgment Day.

Misunderstanding God's Love

Heb. 9:27, *"And as it is appointed unto men once to die, but after this the judgment."*

The Bible says in this verse that we are headed for the courtroom of God. While justice should be present in every courtroom, love has absolutely nothing to do with the functions of a just judge.

There is not a courtroom in the world that begins with the judge asking everyone if they are in love. "Do you attorneys love each other? Do you, the bailiff, love the court reporter? Bailiff, do you love the sheriff's deputy? Deputy, do you love the audience? Audience, do you love the criminal? Criminal, do you love judge?"

That is never done because love is irrelevant in that situation. Love has no place in a courtroom at all. The purpose of the courtroom is to determine guilt or innocence and, if guilt is determined, to set punishment. That is the purpose of the courtroom.

So to go through life with the knowledge that God loves me and, therefore, everything is going to be all right on Judgment Day because He loves me is a false assumption.

Imagine this:

A woman you love dearly (mother, sister, daughter) has been brutally raped and murdered. The police have captured the person who has done it, and he has made an open confession. Several witnesses put him at the scene of the crime. DNA evidence links him to the tragedy. He is, without a doubt, the killer.

Imagine then going through the emotional trauma of the funeral.

Next see yourself going to the trial day after day, reading and watching the media and living for the moment when you will hear the judge condemn the criminal to die.

The jury returns to the courtroom. The audience is asked to stand. The emotions of gratefulness and sense of justice rise in your heart. You sit back down, waiting with joy for the words that you have longed to hear.

But what if, at this moment, the judge asks the criminal if he has anything to say. What if, to your horror, the convict stands and says, "Your honor, I have fully admitted I raped and murdered this woman in cold blood. I have freely admitted that I am the murderer that everyone has accused me of being. But, your honor, there is something else that I know. I have lived in this town all of my life. I know I have only raped once and murdered once. I know there are plenty of people in this town who have raped more than one person; murdered more than one person. Some have been caught; many of them haven't. I believe that there are plenty of people worse than me in this county. And besides, your honor, I heard that you love everyone in this area. I know that you love me, and besides that,

I'm really genuinely sorry. So would you please let me go now? I have some television programs that I am missing, and I would really rather go and catch up on that and have a meal with my family."

You rise from your seat. Everything within you wants to scream, "Shut up, you fool! Sit down!" But what if, in that horrific moment, the judge has a smile gracing his face. He slams the gavel down and says, "You're right. How could I have been so foolish? I am a judge who loves. I am a judge who forgives. You are free to go. After all, you're right. There are plenty of people who are worse than you, and you said you are sorry!"

If the above scenario were true, you would scream for justice to be done. You would lunge for the man's throat as he left the courtroom. Why? Simply put, you know that justice has not been served and that love has nothing to do with a courtroom. Justice is supposed to be done there.

So in the eternal courtroom of God - as it is appointed to man once to die, and after that the judgment - love will have no place. It will be about guilt and innocence. God, certainly being a just judge, will not let the guilty escape without punishment! How could God allow liars, rapists, murderers, and a proud heart to enter into the Kingdom of Heaven? Are we so bold on the earth today as to think that a holy God would have a lesser sense of justice than an earthly judge? God's love is great, but only on this side of the grave.

CHAPTER SIX

Lie #6:

"The people I know are too hard."

When Christians believe the "lie" that sinners around them or abroad are too hardened, they are simply denying the power of the Holy Spirit to change and save a soul.

Consider the characters of the Bible. Moses, raised in the palace away from all righteous and godly instruction, murders a man, and spends forty years on the backside of a desert. Then he has a radical encounter with God and begins his walk and ministry with God at the age of eighty!

Consider Saul of Tarsus. Saul was a religious man who, according to scripture, hated Christianity. He hated Jesus so much that he was willing to give his entire career to the imprisonment and death of those who followed what he believed to be a false and blasphemous messiah.

Though man is limited in his efforts, sincere and well-planned as they may be, the Holy Spirit is all power, all wisdom, and all strength. The Bible says that it is *"Not by might, nor by power, but by my spirit saith the Lord of hosts."* (Zechariah 4:6)

Having traveled to some twenty nations of the earth, I can testify that every legitimate Christian church has righteous, holy, and on-fire-for-God members who were once classified by those who knew them as "too hard, too far gone, or too impossible to reach for Christ."

If the Bible teaches us anything, it teaches that God delights in doing the impossible! Many Christians around the world testify to seeing their own family members saved, and today living a productive Christian life. These are Christians who reluctantly admit that they lived for weeks, months, and years believing that others could be saved, but their own inner circle was too hard.

Think for a moment. Have you been guilty of such a pattern of thinking? Have you ever been in a church service when someone stood to intercede for the lost, asking you to join in faith for your own family and unsaved loved ones? Have you ever caught yourself at that moment saying something like "What's the point? They are too far gone. They're too hard"?

The Bible says that a prophet is without honor in his own country. I believe the reverse principle is sometimes true. Christians sometimes believe that the sinners closest to them are the hardest sinners of all, and are, therefore, not likely to be saved at all.

Since Satan is a liar and the Father of all lies, how much more must he try to deceive Christians by convincing them that those who may really be close to salvation are too far gone to be saved. Satan does this to cause Christians to cease their evangelistic efforts.

Let us renew our faith again in the Lord of the harvest since He said Himself that *"the fields are white as unto the harvest."* This harvest includes your family, friends, and associates. Remind yourself that without faith, it is impossible for us to please Him.

Jesus' death provided salvation for "whosoever will," so the

Gospel is available for all who will reach for it. Remember, the Bible tells us that the very Gospel itself is the POWER of God unto salvation. There is POWER in simply proclaiming the Gospel message. Your inner circle can be the next names God writes in The Book of Life.

Don't allow Satan's lies to cause your faith to stumble. Remember, *"All things are possible to him that believeth."* (Mark 9:23)

LIE#7:

"Lost people are miserable and unhappy."

I *hear it everywhere.*

I hear it often.

I hear it regularly.

...from Christian media to the American pulpit and those around the world. The message seldom changes. Jesus Christ is offered as a solution to the problems of this generation. In short, *Jesus is offered as the greatest life enhancement tool of all time.*

Listen to most popular preaching and you will hear something like this:

- Are you lonely? Jesus will give you a friend.
- Do you need money? Jesus will prosper you.
- Are you hurting? Jesus wants to heal you.
- Do you have a bad marriage? He'll heal that marriage.
- Do you have a rebellious son? God will bring him home and restore your family.

All of these things are true. Jesus does and will give you all of the above.

BUT THESE ARE BENEFITS OF BEING SAVED, NOT REASONS WHY A SINNER NEEDS TO BE SAVED!

The reason a sinner needs to be saved is plainly spelled out in the Bible. Hebrews 9:27 says, *"It is appointed unto men once to die, but after that the judgment."* Romans 6:23 says, *"The wages of sin is death."* Ezekiel 18:4 says, *"The soul that sinneth, it shall die."* Revelation 20:15 says, *"And whosoever was not found written in the book of life was cast into the lake of fire."*

The Bible is very clear. Sinners face the wrath of God on judgment day unless they have been born again on the earth. One weakness with most modern preaching is that the Gospel is presented only to those who are hurting.

This is perhaps one of the most misunderstood issues facing the church today. The very simple fact of the matter is that, while there are thousands, even millions, caught in the clutches of sin whose lives are literally like hell on earth, there are equally millions who are enjoying the life of sin for a season. They are not unhappy. They are not miserable. They are not lonely. They are not depressed. They are having the time of their lives, and to suggest otherwise is to completely deny both the Bible and reality.

Hebrews 11:25 warns us there is *pleasure* in sin, but only for a season. The Bible does not give a time frame of what a "season" is composed of. For many, it will be years, even decades. For others, it will be just hours.

For Christians to keep assuming that all sinners are miserable and unhappy is to guarantee that many will not be interested in what the church of Jesus Christ has to say.

Is there pleasure in sin for years? Ask Hugh Hefner, the multimillionaire founder of *Playboy* Magazine who has enjoyed health, wealth, fame, and beautiful women. Tell him that he is having a miserable life. I'd like to see his reaction.

In our culture, it has become important for Christians to think that all sinners are miserable. But as we have just pointed out, the Bible clearly teaches otherwise. While the length of "a season" is different for different people, clearly the Bible says that *SIN IS FUN!*

Imagine walking out on the streets in any neighborhood in any city and approaching a nineteen-year-old male who is having regular sex with his girlfriend. The young man is in good health. He has good looks and is admired by both his family and friends for his talents and what he will surely achieve and become one day. His parents make his car payments. He has free access to all the video games and latest electronic gadgets. He buys enough drugs to get an occasional recreational high with his friends. And he has cleverly arranged for an older brother to purchase liquor for him for his weekend partying time.

Now tell this young man that he needs to stop having sex with his girlfriend and wait until he is married, which could be several more years! Then tell him that he needs to stop staying out late on Saturday night and give up rated R-rated movies, alcohol and drugs. Tell him that he needs to get rid of 99% of the music that he listens to, stop watching 99% of all the movies and shows that he watches, and get rid of 99% of his friends. Then he needs to get up early on Sunday mornings, giving up his sleeping time, go to a building he's never been in and "worship" with people he has never known, doesn't like, and doesn't care about. In addition, he will need to selflessly give 10% of his lifetime income away. Tell that guy to come on out and go to church with you and that he doesn't know what "fun" he is missing!

The Problem

The problem with presenting the Gospel to only those who are hurting is that obviously those who are not hurting are simply not interested. Thus, by taking to the pulpit, airwaves, and print of today's Christian evangelistic thrust, all those who are not "caught up in miserable sin" have no need of the Gospel.

Imagine being a bottled water salesman and marketing your product strictly to those who are "dying of thirst." Would *most* people in today's society be interested? Are *most* people you know on the brink of dehydration and/or a heat stroke? Of course not. However, we know that every person who goes more than 7 days without water is going to die. So, if you were to present your product as being necessary for their very health and survival, so whether they want water or not, or they feel like they need water or not, you show them that water is something they MUST have. Now who is interested? All those who are concerned about their health. A much larger audience.

The Bible doesn't say, "Without happiness no man will see the Lord."

It doesn't say, "Those who are miserable will automatically get a ticket to Heaven and those who are happy will get an automatic ticket to Hell." It says, "Without holiness, no man will see the Lord."

The Bible cuts through the emotional ties of it. Let's face it. *There are plenty of unhappy Christians and there are plenty of happy sinners.*

The bottom line is that it is appointed unto us once to die and after that our judgment day. We simply cannot afford to face God in our sins or the wrath of God will sentence us and condemn us to eternity in the lake of fire. Doesn't it make sense to present man's need for the Gospel in this fashion?

If we truly want to be the effective Christians Christ died for us to be, let us once and for all present ourselves to God, resisting the devil and his lies and watch as he flees from us on a daily basis.

Allow the Holy Spirit to fill you now with a new sense of urgency to reach the lost, and recommit yourself to spending the rest of your life preaching God's law to the proud, and proclaiming His grace to the humble.

WOULD GOD CALL YOU A CHRISTIAN?

The word "Christian" is perhaps the most misused word in the English language. Many people consider themselves to be Christians and yet have no idea what the word means, involves, or implies. Simply assuming that one is a Christian is not safe because it is possible to be both sincere and wrong.

The Bible shows us what a Christian's life will look like, so it makes sense to see if the One who authored the Bible would call us Christians. Please honestly examine yourself by answering the following questions. I John 5:13 says, *"I write these things that you may know you have eternal life."*

1. Do you claim to be a Christian but live in intentional sin?
"If we say that we have fellowship with Him, and walk in darkness, we lie, and do not the truth" (I John 1:16).

2. Do you keep God's commandments?
"And hereby we do know that we know Him, if we keep His commandments. He that saith, I know Him and keepeth not His commandments is a liar, and the truth is not in him" (I John 2:3,4).

3. Do you hate anyone?

"He that saith he is in the light, and hateth his brother, is in darkness even until now. If a man say, I love God, and hateth his brother, he is a liar: for he that loveth not his brother whom he has seen, how can he love God whom he hath not seen?" (I John 2:9, 4:20).

4. Do you love this world and the "things" that are in the world?

"Love not the world, neither the things that are in the world. If any man love the world, the love of the Father is not in him" (I John 4:15).

5. If you have heard the Gospel before, have you always lived for God? Or have you always done the things that you know are right?

"Let that therefore abide in you, which ye have heard from the beginning. If that which ye have heard from the beginning shall remain in you, ye shall continue in the Son, and in the Father" (I John 2:24).

Did you answer "yes" to one or more of these questions? Perhaps you're still unsure. Let's look at another "mirror" that God has placed for us in His word: the Ten Commandments. Answer "yes" or "no" to these:

1. Has God always been first in your life?
2. Have you ever shaped a god to suit your beliefs?
3. Have you ever taken God's name in vain?
4. Have you always gone to church and kept the Sabbath holy?
5. Have you always honored your father and mother?
6. Have you ever murdered? (The Bible says hatred is the same as murder.)
7. Have you ever committed adultery? (The Bible says lust of the

heart is the same thing.)
8. Have you ever stolen?
9. Have you ever lied?
10. Have you ever coveted (desired) what belongs to someone else?

As we can see, the God of the Bible demands a much higher standard than man. James 2:10 says, *"For whosoever shall keep the whole law, and yet offend in one point, he is guilty of all."*

The God of Scripture takes the word "Christian" very seriously. Merely claiming oneself to be a Christian doesn't make it so any more than going to a supermarket makes someone a bag of groceries. The Bible tells us in Hebrews 9:27, *"And as it is appointed unto men once to die, but after this the judgment."* This means that you will stand before God one day and only what He says about your life will matter.

We Can Be Sure

Because God loves us and desired to save us from the consequences of our disobedience (eternal Hell), Jesus Christ came into the world and suffered and died on the cross for our sins. We broke His commandments; He paid the fine. Then He rose from the dead and defeated death, so that we could repent (turn from our sins and turn to God) and be saved.

Why not give your life to Christ now? The Bible tells us that God is not willing that any should perish, but that all should come to repentance. If you repent and put your faith in Jesus Christ as Lord and Savior, God will give you everlasting life.

If you are ready to turn from sin and put your faith in Jesus, pray something like this:

Dear Jesus, I am a sinner. I have broken your commandments.

If I died as I am, I would be guilty and end up in hell. Your Word says if any one comes to you, you will not cast them aside. I ask you now, forgive me of all my sins. Be my Lord, and my Savior. I renounce all of my past. Fill me with your Holy Spirit. Show me your will for my life. In your precious name... Amen.

If you have prayed that prayer for the first time or if you are a backslider coming back to God, write me for a free book on how you can grow as a new Christian. When you write, be sure to include your prayer requests!! Write to:

Mike Smalley
Worldreach Ministries
P. O. Box 99
Rockwall, TX 75087
or e-mail us at revjms@hotmail.com

Visit our web site at www.mikesmalley.com

ABOUT THE AUTHOR

Called to preach at age 14, Mike Smalley has a burden for lost people. Mike is the founder of Worldreach Ministries near Dallas, Texas, which plants churches and conducts crusades worldwide, in addition to training Christians in evangelism. Mike has travelled to over 15 nations and has started 11 churches throughout various parts of Africa. His ministry crosses denominational lines and boundaries to take the Gospel where it is needed most.

If you would like more information about Mike Smalley and Worldreach Ministries and its other ministry resources, or to invite Mike to speak in your area, write to:

Worldreach Ministries
P.O. Box 99
Rockwall, TX 75087

Or, call:
(972)771-3339

Or, you can visit Mike on the web:
www.mikesmalley.com